How to say French words

French is pronounced differently from English – almost always at the front of the mouth, using the tip of the tongue.

j in French is said like a soft *z*, or rather *zh*. **Je** means I and you pronounce it *zhuh*. **Je suis** is I am, pronounced *zhuh swee*.

If you see the letters **eau** or **eaux** together, they are pronounced *oh*. In French, **château** (a castle) is pronounced *shat-oh*.

eu is said like *err* in English. So if you ask for **deux** (two) of something, you say *derr*, as in the English word 'under'. You often see words ending in 'er'. This

is pronounced like the English word 'air'. So **lever**, meaning to lift, is pronounced *lev-air*.

Except in a few special cases, the French do not sound 's' at the end of a word. If you see **les toilettes** (the toilets) you say *lay twah-lett*, not *lay twah-letts*.

The letter 'n' is a bit difficult for English speakers! Imagine you are saying the letters 'ng' quickly, so that the 'g' is almost silent, as in 'bang'. 'Good' in French is **bon** but you say it like *bong*.

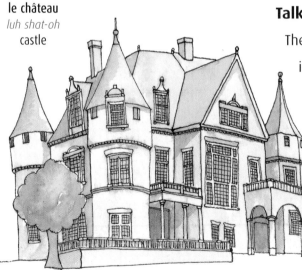

le château
luh shat-oh
castle

Talking to other people

There are two different words for 'you' in French. You use **tu** if you are speaking to people you know well, but you say **vous** (*voo*) to someone you don't know very well. Children usually use **tu** when they talk to each other.

4

D0229421

î

say *ee*

à

say *ah*

ç

say *es*

é

say *ay*

Masculine and feminine words

In French, all nouns are either masculine or feminine. **Le salon** (the living room) is masculine. **La porte** (the door) is feminine. If there is more than one, however, 'the' becomes **les** whether the word is masculine or feminine – e.g. **Les portes** – the doors.

Accents

Sometimes letters have an accent under or over them. They are pronounced differently (see above). If you see the letter **ç** like this, it is pronounced 's' as in sock, not 'c' as in cat.

Vowels

e is pronounced *a*

a is pronounced like a short *ah*

i is pronounced like a short *e*

le salon
luh sal-ong
the living room

la porte
lah port
the door

la chaise
lah shayz
the chair

la table
lah tar-bluh
the table

An accent over a letter tells you to make the sound longer.

Introduction

A journey around France **5**

Paris and the big cities **8**

Sports **12**

Find out what French people do in their spare time.

Did you know?

👍 The Eiffel Tower has 2.5 million rivets, 15,000 pieces of iron, more than 40 tons of paint and 1,652 steps.

👍 Paris has over 70 museums, monuments and other cultural attractions.

👍 The Louvre Museum in Paris is home to the Mona Lisa by Leonardo da Vinci, the most famous painting in the world.

👍 The Mona Lisa has been part of France's Royal collection since the early 16th century.

👍 5.5 million people visit the Eiffel Tower every year.

👍 The lowest point in France is the Rhône river delta at 2m below sea level.

👍 There are 36,851 towns and villages in France, including its overseas territories.

👍 The Channel Tunnel linked Britain and France by land for the first time since the Ice Age.

👍 In Paris you are never more than 400 m from the nearest Metro Station.

👍 The actual height of the Eiffel Tower is 300 m, but it grows by 15 cm in the summer as the metal expands and then shrinks again when it cools in the winter.

A journey around France

The capital of France is Paris but the country has 22 regions, each with its own customs, way of life and food. French is the main language but Bréton is spoken in the northwest region, Brittany. In the southwest, Gascony uses the Basque language and a dialect, part French and part German, is spoken in Alsace-Lorraine in the northeast.

The French have developed the best railway system in Europe to link the regions. Their high-speed trains are called **TGVs**, which is short for **trains à grande vitesse**. A **TGV** set the world speed record for trains in 1990, going at 515 kmph. **TGVs** go to 200 different places in France.

There is a good network of internal flights by Air France and foreign airlines. Nearly all French cities, even quite small ones, have their own airport.

France also has superb motorways, called **autoroutes**, although you must pay a toll at the **péage** (*pay-ahzh*) to use them. Payment is linked to the number of kilometres you have travelled on the *autoroutes*.

The French are very keen on the internet, which about 22 million of them already use regularly, and there are 42 million mobile phone users. Both figures are growing all the time.

Motorway toll

How many TGV trains (called 'trainsets') are in operation on French railways today?

Paris is a beautiful city with plenty of entertaining things to do and see – from Disneyland Paris to galleries and museums, to pavement cafés and restaurants, where you can enjoy a drink and watch the world go by. But France is also one of the least crowded countries in Europe, so why not pack your bags and go by train, car or air to explore the countryside and sights beyond Paris?

Chartres is not far from the capital, for example, and has one of the oldest and most impressive Gothic cathedrals in the world. If you travel southeast beyond Grenoble, you will find some of Europe's highest mountains and best skiing resorts, such as Megève, Courchevel and Chamonix.

Chartres Cathedral

Horse riding

The Alps

6

Visit www.megeve.com/webcams_gb/ to see the view from the top of the mountain.

Horse riding is a popular sport and there are opportunities to try it all over France, but the best region is the Camargue, a flat, windy, wild area in the southwest. Here you will find the famous white horses and the bulls of the region.

If you travel on to Provence you will find deep gorges and more mountains. You may see eagles and, if you are very lucky, wild boar. By contrast, you will also see great fields of lavender, grown around places like Grasse and Puimoisson, for use in making perfumes. Then on to the coast and famous seaside resorts such as Nice, Antibes and St Tropez where you can paraglide, windsurf or just enjoy the beaches.

Beach in the south

Fields of lavender

Windsurfing

7

Which southern seaside town has an important film festival every year?

Paris and the big cities

Two thousand years ago, the Roman name for Paris was Lutetia. Today, more than 10 million people live in the capital, which is one of the world's most famous and popular cities.

Arc de Triomphe

Sacré-Coeur

Even today, when it has become crowded and expensive, artists and writers find Paris an exciting place to live and work – you may see them arguing with each other at a pavement café!

Artist and model

Eiffel Tower

8

Marseilles *(mar-say)*, on the south coast, is the biggest commercial port in France and, with a million inhabitants, overtook Lyon in 1990 to become France's second biggest city. The old harbour is very picturesque. People of many different ethnic backgrounds – particularly from North Africa – live and work in Marseilles, which is divided into a hundred districts, called *quartiers*.

At the market

Picking grapes

Lyon *(lee-ong)* has been an important city for over two thousand years. This is where travellers cross two big rivers, the Rhône *(rown)* and the Saône *(sah-own)*, which meet in the centre of Lyon. When Germany invaded France in 1940, Lyon was one of the first cities it captured. As a result, the French Resistance here was particularly fierce. Two of the best-known winemaking areas are near Lyon – Beaujolais *(bo-zhol-ay)* to the north and Côtes du Rhône *(coat-doo-rown)* to the south.

Lille *(leel)*, is northern France's largest city. It was once a major industrial centre and went into decline in the 1950s. Today it has transformed itself into a banking and educational centre. It was Culture Capital of Europe in 2004.

Grand Place, Lille

Go to www.marseille-tourisme.com to see how many people visit each year.

Other important cities in France

Bordeaux *(bor-doh)* is the fifth largest city in France, with beautiful 18th-century buildings around the Esplanade des Quinconces and along the waterfront. It has been a busy Atlantic port at the mouth of the river Garonne for over two thousand years. Bordeaux is surrounded by world-famous vineyards, and you can visit many of the wine-producing estates with famous names such as Margaux, Latour, Pauillac and St Emilion.

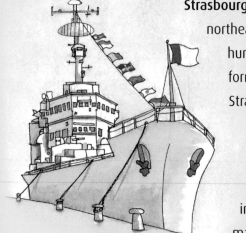

Strasbourg *(straz-borg)* is the capital of Alsace-Lorraine in the northeast. France and Germany have fought over it for hundreds of years, so when the European Union was formed the European Parliament was placed in Strasbourg as a sign of future peace.

Toulouse *(too-looz)* is France's fourth city, and the largest in the southeast of the country. It was founded by the Romans and today it is a busy industrial and university centre. The presence of so many students means that prices in the shops and cafés never get too high!

Navy ship, Brest

Pont de Pierre, Bordeaux

 Put Toulouse into your search engine to find out what the airport is called.

Toulouse is at the heart of Europe's aviation industry. The Anglo-French *Concorde*, the world's only supersonic airliner, was developed and tested here in the 1960s and 1970s. The *Ariane* space rocket was also developed in Toulouse and these days it is the home of the Airbus, whose planes are as well known as the American Boeings.

Concorde

Southeast of Toulouse you can visit a huge space park called the Cité de l'espace. It has a planetarium, interactive exhibitions about the exploration of space, a terradome showing films about the history of the earth and a section where you can learn how to launch rockets and satellites.

Brest, on the most westerly tip of France, is another major seaport and is the home of the French navy. Europe's largest lifting bridge crosses the river Penfeld and you will also find Océanopolis in Brest. It is an entertaining sea centre with three large pavilions for temperate, tropical and polar marine life. Not far away the fearsome Pointe de Raz sticks out into the Atlantic ocean, with pounding seas breaking over jagged rocks.

European Parliament, Strasbourg

Visit www.oceanopolis.com to find out how much seawater the centre needs.

Sports

The French are enthusiastic sportsmen and women. Although they like popular sports such as football, they also enjoy playing *boules* (or *pétanque*) in town and village squares all over the country.

France won football's World Cup, held every four years, in 1998, when it beat Brazil 3-0. It lost in the 2006 final to Italy. Rugby is also very strong, particularly in Paris and the south-west and France is the host for the Rugby World Cup in 2007.

But the French also love unusual sports. Apart from *boules*, bullfighting is popular in the south. France also has outstanding mountaineers and skiers.

Playing boules

France has also produced many great sailors and the famous single-handed Vendée Globe nonstop-around-the-world yacht race was founded by a Frenchman and is often won by a Frenchman.

In summer you will see cyclists everywhere, dreaming of being another Lance Armstrong and winning the celebrated Tour de France – a great test of speed and endurance that lasts three weeks.

Visit www.wikipedia.org to find which five cyclists have won the Tour de France five times.

Life in France

Meet the family **13**

At school **14**

After school **16**

In town **18**

Things people do **20**

Learn useful words and phrases that will help you when you visit France.

Did you know?

👍 The French consume more cheese per person than any other country in the world.

👍 The French republic's official values are Liberty, Equality and Fraternity.

👍 The international dialling code for France is +33; the internet domain is .fr

👍 The emergency numbers in France are 15 for Ambulance, 17 for the Police and 18 for the Fire Brigade. If you dial 112, it will connect you to your local emergency switchboard.

👍 The national medical emergency service in France is called SAMU. It operates 24 hours a day and assists at all sorts of medical emergencies.

👍 France publishes over 100 daily newspapers. They include *Le Monde* and *Le Figaro*.

👍 In the morning, you will often see people drinking their hot chocolate out of bowls into which they can dip their croissants.

👍 French people often have an apéritif, an alcoholic drink, before a meal.

👍 The French have 11 days of holiday (*jours fériés*) each year.

Meet the family

Now it's time to meet the Bernard family. They will introduce you to the kind of life they lead and help you learn some French so you can travel around France more easily.

Nous nous appelons Monsieur et Madame Bernard.
Noo noo zappuh-long Mer-syure ay Mad-ahm Bare-nar.
We are called Mr and Mrs Bernard.

Bienvenue en France!
Bee-ang-ven-oo ong France!
Welcome to France!

Je m'appelle Nicole.
Zhuh map-ell Nick-oll.
My name is Nicole.

Je m'appelle François.
Zhuh map-ell Frong-swa.
My name is François.

François, Nicole and their parents always speak in French. Below is a guide to help you pronounce French correctly and the English is written below that.

Et je m'appelle Nicole - the French words
Ay zhuh map-ell Nick-oll - how to say the French words
And my name is Nicole - what they mean in English

13

The family will tell you about life in France – at home, at school, travelling and having fun.

At school

François and Nicole go to elementary school, which is called *école primaire (ay-col pree-mair)*, for children between 6 and 11 years old. Many schools are now working a four-day week, with Wednesdays off.

School begins around 8:45. There are three hours of lessons in the morning **le matin** *(luh mat-tang)* and another one hour and a half in the afternoon **l'après-midi** *(lap-ray-mee-dee)*.

Nicole and François have a half-hour break in the playground at 10 o'clock. This is called **la récréation** *(lah rek-ray-as-syong)*. In the afternoon there is another half-hour break.

la cour de récréation
lah kor duh rek-ray-ass-yong
playground

les grilles
lay gree
railings

les balançoires
lay bal-on-swah
swings

la fille
lah fee
girl

le cerceau
luh sair-so
hoop

le garçon
luh gahr-song
boy

La pause déjeuner (*lah pows day-zher-nay*) means the lunch break. The children usually have one and a half hours, from 12:30 until 2 p.m., to have their meal and then go out to play.

Classes are called **le cours** (*luh coure*), so if you say **'J'ai un cours'** (*zhay ung coure*), it means 'I have a class' or 'I've got to go to a class'. In an *école primaire*, classes finish at 4 o'clock but it doesn't mean the end of school.

School stays open until 6 o'clock for **l'étude** (*lay-tood*) or 'study'. This means you can do your homework **les devoirs** (*lay der-vwah*) at school if you want to. There is a break for food, called **le goûter** (*ler goo-tay*), which means a snack, between 4:30 and 5:00. But some children prefer to go home for their snack and do **les devoirs** there, and that's allowed. French children have very long school holidays.

l'institutrice
lan-stat-too-trees
teacher

l'élève
lay-lev
pupil

le crayon
luh kray-ong
pencil

le manteau
luh man-toh
coat

le sac
luh sak
bag

le livre
luh leev-rer
book

la table
lah tar-bluh
desk

la salle de classe
lah sal der klass
classroom

After school

François and Nicole can't wait to get home once they have finished their homework. There are so many things to do!

First of all, there are cartoons to watch on television. In French these are called **les dessins animés** *(lay dess-zahn an-nim-may)*. The French are very good at making cartoons and also strip cartoon books, like **Tintin** *(tang-tang)* and **Astérix** *(ass-tair-reeks)*.

After the cartoons, François and Nicole might have a game together, or they might want to do their own things separately.

After a while, François may get out his computer, called **l'ordinateur** *(lor-deen-ah-terr)* in French. Sometimes he plays computer games or **les jeux informatiques** *(lay zhuhr ang-for-mat-eek)*, or he may go on the internet **l'internet** *(lang-tair-net)* to look for information he needs for school. While Nicole waits for her turn at the computer, she reads an *Astérix* story. Sometimes, she does some drawing as she loves making pictures.

The French like to eat well and Madame Bernard takes great care to buy fresh food. As often as she can, she goes to the local market to buy fresh meat, fish, vegetables, cheese and fruit. Mealtimes are important in France and the whole family has dinner – **le dîner** *(luh dee-nay)* – together and talks about the day's events. Eating in front of the television is not allowed!

After dinner, it's time for Nicole to have her bath and go to bed.

l'ordinateur
lor-deen-ah-terr
computer

☞ François and Nicole sleep well. They will have to be up at 7 o'clock for school.

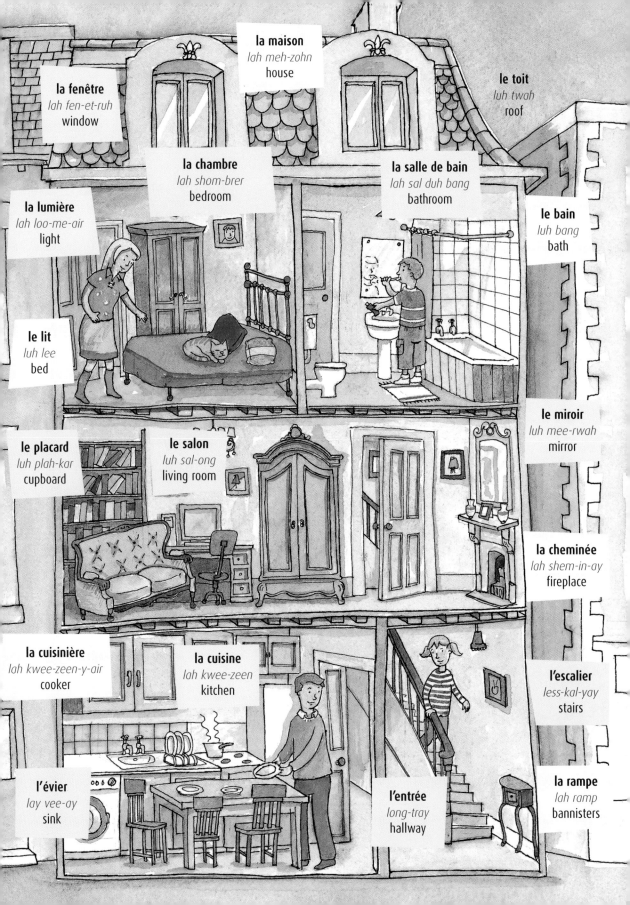

la maison
lah meh-zohn
house

la fenêtre
lah fen-et-ruh
window

le toit
luh twah
roof

la chambre
lah shom-brer
bedroom

la salle de bain
lah sal duh bang
bathroom

le bain
luh bang
bath

la lumière
lah loo-me-air
light

le lit
luh lee
bed

le miroir
luh mee-rwah
mirror

le placard
luh plah-kar
cupboard

le salon
luh sal-ong
living room

la cheminée
lah shem-in-ay
fireplace

la cuisinière
lah kwee-zeen-y-air
cooker

la cuisine
lah kwee-zeen
kitchen

l'escalier
less-kal-yay
stairs

l'évier
lay vee-ay
sink

l'entrée
long-tray
hallway

la rampe
lah ramp
bannisters

In town

It's the weekend – *le weekend!* François and Nicole love the weekend because there's no school. Monsieur Bernard doesn't have to go to work. But for Madame Bernard it's often the busiest time of the week.

la mairie
lah mair-ree
the town hall

la pâtisserie
lah pat-ees-ser-ee
bakery

la maison de la presse
lah meh-zohn duh lah press
newsagent

la poste
lah posst
post office

la banque
lah bohnk
the bank

le trottoir
luh trot-wah
pavement

l'avion
lah-viong
aeroplane

la pharmacie
lah farm-ass-ee
the chemist

la librairie
lah lee-brair-ree
the bookshop

l'épicerie
lay-pee-ser-ee
the grocer

le supermarché
luh soop-air-mar-shay
the supermarket

le garage
luh gah-rarzh
petrol station

Mme Bernard goes to the stores, while M Bernard fills his car with petrol at the petrol station in town.

le pêcheur
luh pay-sher
fisherman

There are usually three types of place to eat: restaurants, bistros and cafés. Bistros are informal and you can have moderately priced traditional food. Cafés offer simple snacks such as omelettes and salads.

The people of Brittany (called Bretons) are mainly farmers and fishermen. Nearly half of all the fish caught in the sea around France comes from this northwest region.

Today, cars, aeroplanes, nuclear plants, telecommunications equipment, food and wine are some of the main exports of France.

Many French people work in hotels and restaurants. The tourist trade is very important, especially in the south and in the mountains to the east. But French families also eat out often and enjoy going to restaurants.

People everywhere love French food. It is considered to be among the best in the world.

Facts about France

50 French history facts **23**

Famous people **27**

Things to see **31**

50 facts about France **35**

part three

Did you know?

👍 King Henry III, Louis XVI and Napoleon all suffered from ailurophobia, a fear of cats.

👍 France still has 16 territories under its jurisdiction, including French Polynesia, Martinique, New Caledonia and Guadeloupe.

👍 The Bayeaux tapestry is a 70 m long embroidered work that depicts the Norman invasion of England in 1066. It is on display in Normandy in northern France.

👍 Louis Braille (1809-1853) invented the system of dots that blind people use to read.

👍 Gustave Eiffel, who built the tower in Paris, was also the structural engineer for the Statue of Liberty in New York.

👍 Marie Curie was the first woman to win a Nobel Prize.

👍 The Entente Cordiale was an agreement of friendship signed by France and Britain in 1904.

👍 To date, four competitors have died while cycling in the Tour de France.

👍 There is a museum in Paris devoted to sewers.

50 French history facts

1 **About 15,000 B.C.** Cave paintings are done by prehistoric men at Lascaux and Les Eyzies in central France.

2 **58-51 B.C.** Julius Caesar conquers Gaul, as France is then called. It becomes part of the Roman Empire.

3 **800 A.D.** The third King of France, Charlemagne, becomes Holy Roman Emperor.

Charlemagne

4 **1337-1453** The Hundred Years' War between England and France. England wins the battles of Crécy (1346), Poitiers (1356) and Agincourt (1415) before the French emerge victorious and drive the English out of nearly all of France.

5 **1348** The Black Death, a fatal disease, sweeps through France. It kills about one-third of the population of Europe and is followed by several years of famine.

6 **1431** Joan of Arc is burned at the stake in Rouen by the English. She later becomes a French national hero and is made a saint.

7 **1539** French is made the official language of the country, replacing Latin. Before World War II, French was considered the international language for diplomacy.

8 **1562-1593** Bitter wars of religion rage between Catholics and Protestants. In 1572, there is a massacre of Protestants in Paris.

Protestant murdered

9 **1631** The first newspaper in France is published, called *La Gazette*. It continues to exist until 1917.

10 **1668** Louis XIV (The Sun King) begins the expansion of the Palace of Versailles, which becomes the official residence of the kings of France.

The Sun King

11 **1783** The first manned balloon flight is made by de Rozier and Laurent. They fly $5^{1}/_{2}$ miles over Paris in 25 minutes in a hot air balloon built by the Montgolfier brothers and reach a height of about 152 metres.

23

39 **1957** France is one of the founding members of the European Economic Community (the Common Market), together with Italy, Germany, Belgium, Luxembourg and Holland.

40 **1959** In French cinema, the Nouvelle Vague (the New Wave) is launched with the film *Les Quatre Cent Coups (400 Blows)*.

41 **May 1968** A students' revolt breaks out in Paris.

EEC flag

Workers join in the rioting, and France is soon paralysed.

42 **1972** France is divided into its present 22 regions and 96 departments.

47 **1994** The Channel Tunnel is opened, linking England and France for the first time.

Rioting student in 1968

43 **1976** The Anglo-French supersonic airliner, *Concorde*, makes its first commercial flight. Flights continued until 2003.

44 **1977** A revolutionary style of building, the Pompidou Centre, is constructed as an art gallery in Paris.

45 **1989** To mark the bicentenary of the French Revolution, La Grande Arche is opened in the modernist La Défense business area of Paris.

46 **1991** Edith Cresson becomes the first woman prime minister of France and holds office for less than a year.

48 **1998** France wins the football World Cup, defeating Brazil.

49 **1999** The new European currency, the euro, is adopted by France to replace the French franc.

Euros

50 **2006** Opening by President Chirac of the Musée du Quai Branly, the first major museum to open in Paris since 1986. It is devoted entirely to non-Western art and civilisations.

 Go to www.map-of-france.co.uk to find out what the 22 regions of France are called.

Famous people

Leaders

Charlemagne *(742-814)* became Holy Roman Emperor in 800 A.D.

Joan of Arc

Joan of Arc *(1412-1431)* won the Battle of Orleans against the English in 1429. She was later captured and burned at the stake because the English thought she was a witch!

Louis XIV *(1638-1715)* became king at age 5, and was afterwards known as the Sun King.

Robespierre *(1758-1794)* was a lawyer who became a feared leader of the French Revolution.

Marie Antoinette *(1755-1793)* was the wife of Louis XVI and was sent to the guillotine.

Napoleon *(1769-1821)* was a brilliant soldier who seized power and made himself emperor in 1804.

Clemenceau *(1841-1929)* was prime minister in 1906-09 and 1917-19. Called 'The Tiger' due to his actions in WWI.

Charles de Gaulle *(1890-1970)* organised Free French in World War II. President of France from 1958 to 1969.

Soldiers, sportsmen and explorers

Maréchal Foch *(1851-1929)* was allied supreme commander at the end of WWI.

Maréchal Pétain *(1856-1951)* was a French hero in WWI, but in 1940 made peace with the Germans and was regarded as a traitor.

Pétain

Jacques Anquetil *(1934-1987)* won the Tour de France 5 times between 1957-1964, the first cyclist to achieve this feat.

Jean Borotra *(1898-1994)* was known as the 'Bounding Basque' and one of the four 'French Musketeers' who dominated tennis in the 1920s and 1930s. He is in the International Tennis Hall of Fame in Newport, Rhode Island, USA.

Michel Platini *(b.1955)* soccer player who played for his country 72 times and was made captain of the team in 1984.

27

39 A French mathematician, Blaise Pascal, invented the first mechanical calculator back in 1642!

Eurovision Song Contest

40 The Paris Metro, the first French underground, was opened in 1900. It now has 16 lines.

41 In 1983, the first TGV (*train à grande vitesse*) high-speed train service began running from Paris to Lyon.

42 The TGVs are the world's fastest regular train service. The average speed is 300 kmph.

43 The Channel Tunnel rail link between France and England was opened in 1994. It is 50 km long. Digging it took over seven years.

44 Charles de Gaulle Airport in Paris is the second busiest in Europe (after London's Heathrow), with 51.3 million passengers in 2004.

Metro sign

45 St Bernadette saw a vision of the Virgin Mary at Lourdes in the Pyrenees in 1858.

46 Médecins sans Frontières (Doctors without Borders) is a humanitarian organisation that was created in 1971 by a small group of French doctors. It works mainly in war-torn regions.

47 France has won 12 Nobel Prizes for Literature, the last going to Claude Simon in 1985.

48 St Joan of Arc is the patron saint of France and her feast day is May 30th.

49 For breakfast (*petit déjeuner* - pet-ee day-zhuh-nay) the French prefer *croissants*, made of flaky pastry, or *baguettes* (bread in long, thin loaves) with butter or jam. They usually have *café au lait* (kaf-fay oh lay – coffee with warm milk).

Breakfast

50 The French statesman, Jean Monnet was one of the leaders who created the Common Market (now the European Union) after World War II, and is called the Father of Europe.

France enters the Eurovision Song Contest each year. Find out more at www.eurovision.tv.

Let's learn French!

Speaking French **39**

Meeting people **40**

Making friends **42**

Finding the way **44**

A visit to Paris **46**

Out and about in Paris **48**

Going shopping **50**

Eating out **52**

A day out **54**

Sleepover **56**

The Tour de France **58**

Illness and accidents **60**

Bits of me **61**

Counting **62**

Telling the time **63**

Days, months and seasons **64**

Join Nicole and François on holiday in Paris and learn all about the capital city.

part four

Did you know?

👍 The French language comes from Latin, as do Spanish, English and Italian.

👍 There are around 113 million people worldwide who speak French fluently or as part of their everyday lives.

👍 There are over 35,000 *boulangeries* (bakeries) in France.

👍 The French national anthem is *La Marseillaise*.

👍 The *Marseillaise* was first sung in Strasbourg and not in Marseille as the name suggests.

👍 Francophone *(frank-oh-fone)* means French-speaking.
Une ville francophone means a French-speaking town.

👍 There are 365 different varieties of cheese manufactured in France, one for every day of the year.

👍 99% of the French population can read and write.

👍 The pronunciation of French words is different from the way they are written. That is because French is written as it was spoken four or five centuries ago.

👍 The English language has adopted many French words and phrases into daily use, so you probably already know a few words, such as 'rendezvous'.

Speaking French

When you arrive and hear French people speaking fast you may feel a bit frightened, but it's easier than you think to get started.

Like people everywhere, the French are pleased when you make the effort to speak a few words of their language – just as you would be if someone speaking a foreign language came to your town but had already learned a few words of English. When they see you are trying, they will often smile and try to help you in return - especially outside Paris where they don't see as many foreigners.

s'il vous plaît
see voo play
please

Start with a few simple words like 'hello' or 'good morning' and 'good night'. Always remember to say 'please' and 'thank you'.

Then you can try **ça va?** *(sah-vah?)* with a rising voice to ask 'Is that OK?' when you hand over some money for a postcard or some sweets. If you want something in a shop you can point at it and say **avez-vous un comme ça?** *(av-ay vooz ung kom sah?)*, which means 'Have you got one like that?'

bonjour
bong-jour
good morning

Good to see you again. Are you ready to join Nicole and me to see how we live?

The rest of the book will show you many of the words and phrases you can use to make your stay in France even more enjoyable. Then you can go home feeling you know French people a little better. You'll probably find they enjoy many of the same things you do.

merci
mair-see
thank you

bonne nuit
bong-nwee
good night

39

The next 20 pages will introduce you to the lives of François and Nicole.

Meeting people

French people have different ways of greeting people they meet. They use polite greetings if they do not know the person well. With close friends and family they are less formal.

Monsieur Bernard meets someone he does not know well.

Bonjour, Monsieur Didier.
Bong-joor, Mer-syure Dee-dee-ay.
Good morning, Mr Didier.

Comment allez-vous?
Comm-ong tal-ay voo?
How are you?

Bonjour, Monsieur Bernard.
Bong-joor, Mer-syure Bare-nar.
Good morning, Mr Bernard.

Je vais bien, merci.
Zhe vay be-yang, mair-see.
I'm well, thank you.

François and Nicole go shopping with their mother and meet some friends.

Salut. Ça va, Nicole?
Sal-oo. Sah vah, Nick-oll?
Hello. Everything OK, Nicole?

Ça va, merci, et toi?
Sah vah, mair-see, ay twah?
Fine, thanks, and you?

A bientôt.
Ah bee-yang-toe.
See you soon.

40

Monsieur Bernard welcomes visitors to his home for dinner.

Bonsoir! Entrez, s'il vous plaît.
Bong-swah! On-tray see voo play.
Good evening! Please come in.

Bonne nuit, Maman.
Bong nwee, mam-ahng.
Good night, Mummy.

Bonne nuit, Nicole. Dors bien.
Bong-nwee, Nick-oll. Dor bee-yang.
Good night, Nicole. Sleep well.

Bonjour is used to greet people during the daytime and *bonsoir* in the evenings.
Bonne nuit (good night) is used only the last thing at night.

When people meet, they often like to discuss the weather.

Bonjour, madame. Il fait beau aujourd'hui, n'est-ce pas?
Bong-joor, mad-arm. Eel fay boh oh-joord-wee, ness-pah?
Good day, madam. It's a lovely day, isn't it?

Oui, il fait très chaud.
Wee, eel fay tray shoh.
Yes, it's very warm.

41

Making friends

The Bernard family has gone into the country for a picnic by a big lake. After lunch, François and Nicole run off to play football on the grass while their parents sunbathe.

Salut. Je m'appelle Pierre. Comment vous appellez vous?
Sal-oo. Zhe map-ell Pee-air. Comm-ong voo-zap-lay voo?
Hello. My name is Pierre. What are your names?

Bonjour. Je m'appelle François, et ma soeur s'appelle Nicole.
Bong-joor. Zhuh map-ell Frong-swa, ay mah soo-er sap-ell Nick-oll.
Hello. I am François and my sister is called Nicole.

Salut, Pierre. Quel âge as-tu?
Sal-oo, Pee-air. Kell ahj ah-too?
Hello, Pierre. How old are you?

J'ai dix ans.
Zhay dee zong.
I am ten.

Tu habites où, Pierre?
Too ab-eat oo, Pee-air?
Where do you live, Pierre?

J'habite à Paris. Nous sommes en vacances ici.
Zhab-eet ah Pah-ree. Noo soms ong vack-ons ee-see.
I live in Paris. We are on holiday here.

Pierre introduces his friend from England.

The rest of the Bernard family enjoys sitting in the sun.

Finding the way

François and Nicole go to the nearby town with their new friends, Pierre and Tom. They look for the park while their parents go shopping.

Helpful words and phrases for asking the way:

à gauche
ah gohsh
on the left

là-bas
lah-bah
over there

en face de
ong fass duh
opposite

44

 à côté de *ah koh-tay duh* next to (or beside) • **derrière** *dare-ree-air* behind

On the way back to the car park where their parents left them, the children get lost.

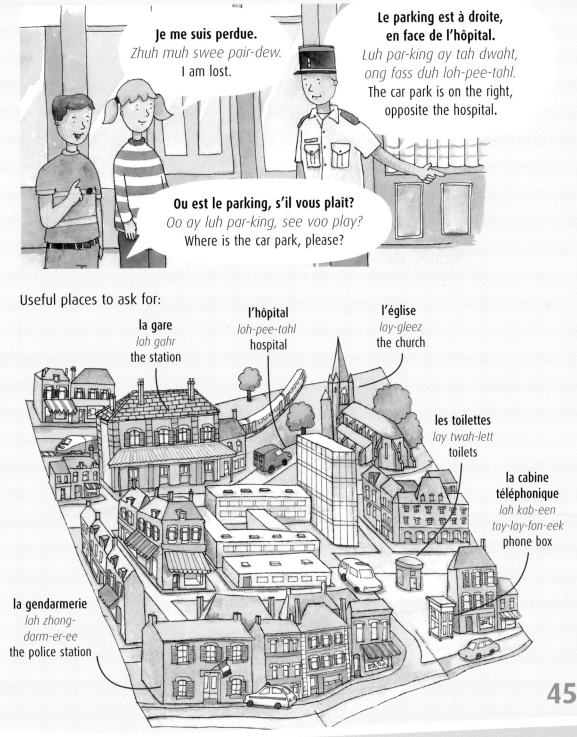

Je me suis perdue.
Zhuh muh swee pair-dew.
I am lost.

Le parking est à droite, en face de l'hôpital.
Luh par-king ay tah dwaht, ong fass duh loh-pee-tahl.
The car park is on the right, opposite the hospital.

Ou est le parking, s'il vous plaît?
Oo ay luh par-king, see voo play?
Where is the car park, please?

Useful places to ask for:

la gare
lah gahr
the station

l'hôpital
loh-pee-tahl
hospital

l'église
lay-gleez
the church

les toilettes
lay twah-lett
toilets

la cabine téléphonique
lah kab-een tay-lay-fon-eek
phone box

la gendarmerie
lah zhong-darm-er-ee
the police station

45

jusqu'à *joo-skah* as far as ● devant *der-vong* in front of ● entre *ong-truh* between

A visit to Paris

Pierre's parents have asked the Bernards to visit them in Paris. François has been there once before but Nicole has never seen Paris. They are staying in a hotel.

Nous avons réservé deux chambres au nom de Bernard.
Noo zav-ong rez-air-vay duh shom-bruh oh nom der Bare-nar.
We have reserved two rooms in the name of Bernard.

Ah oui. Vous avez les numéros cinq et six.
Ah wee. Voo zav-ay lay noom-er-oh sank ay seece.
Ah yes. You have numbers five and six.

Voici vos clefs, monsieur.
Vwah-see vo klay, Mer-syure.
Here are your keys, sir.

À quelle heure est le petit déjeuner?
Ah kell err ay luh pet-ti day-zher-nay?
What time is breakfast?

À partir de sept heures, madame.
Ah part-ear duh sett err, mad-ahm.
From seven o'clock on, madam.

François and Nicole are very excited. They can't wait to go and explore Paris with their parents.

**Regarde, François.
Voilà la Tour Eiffel!**
*Rer-gard, Frong-swa.
Vwah-lah lah Too-er Ee-fel!*
Look, François. There's
the Eiffel Tower!

C'est énorme!
Say ten-orm!
It's enormous!

Some of the sights of Paris:

Place de la
Concorde

Palais du Louvre

Champs Elysées

47

Out and about in Paris

Not only is Paris the capital of France but it is also the centre of industry, business, fashion and entertainment. The Bernard family is going to meet Pierre's family at a café.

> **Je voudrais prendre le metro.**
> *Zhuh voo-dray prong-druhr luh met-roh.*
> I would like to go on the metro.

> **Moi aussi. S'il te plaît, Papa!**
> *Mwah oh-see. See-ter-play, pah-pah!*
> Me too. Please, Daddy!

They are waiting in the station for the train.

> **Nous devons descendre au troisième arrêt.**
> *Noo der-vong day-son-drer oh twah-ze-aimar-ret.*
> We need (to get out at) the third stop.

> **Le train arrive tout de suite!**
> *Luh trang ar-reev toot-sweet!*
> The train is coming now!

There isn't enough time to visit all the sights in a city as big as Paris. Before they set off to explore, they visit a café.

Alors, un café, un thé, une limonade et un coca, s'il vous plaît.
Al-lor, ung kaf-ay, ung tay, oon lee-mon-ahd ay ung koke-a, see-voo-play.
Okay, one coffee, one tea, a lemonade and a Coke, please.

Bien sûr, madame. Vous desirez un café noir ou un café au lait?
Bee-ang sewr, mad-ahm. Voo day-zir-ay ung kaf-ay nwah oo ung kaf-ay oh lay?
Certainly, madam. Do you want black coffee or coffee with milk?

the oldest bridge in Paris

Le pont neuf

the smartest shopping street in Paris

La rue de Rivoli

49

La place de la Bastille *(lah plass duh lah Bas-steel)* is where the French Revolution started in 1789.

Going shopping

Paris is the centre of fashion so Madame Bernard wants to look at dresses and hats and perhaps some shoes.

Cette robe est très jolie.
Set rob ay tray zhol-ee.
This dress is very pretty.

Je voudrais l'essayer.
Zhuh voo-dray less-ay-yay.
I would like to try it on.

Bien sûr, madame.
Bee-yang sewr, mad-ahm.
Certainly, madam.

Par ici, s'il vous plaît.
Par ee-see, see-voo-play.
Come this way, please.

François, Nicole and their mother and father go to the news stand on the corner.

Combien coûtent les cartes postales?
Com-bee-yang koot lay kart poss-tahl?
How much are the postcards?

Et ces deux tablettes de chocolat?
Ay say duh tab-let duh shok-oh-lah?
And these two chocolate bars?

There are very good, colourful markets in Paris and in most French towns and villages. These are some of the things you will see in them.

les artichauts
layz ar-tee-show
artichokes

les tomates
lay tom-aht
tomatoes

les choux
lay shoo
cabbages

les pommes de terre
lay pom-duh-tair
potatoes

les poires
lay pwahr
pears

les carottes
lay car-ott
carrots

**Je voudrais un journal,
s'il vous plaît.**
*Zhuh voo-dray ung zhoor-nahl,
see-voo-play.*
I would like a
newspaper, please.

**Trois euros les chocolats.
Chaque carte coûte soixante cents.**
*Twah zerr-oh lay shok-oh-lah.
Shak cart koot swah-song sents.*
Three euros for the chocolate.
Each card is sixty cents.

51

Eating out

It will soon be time for the Bernard family to leave Paris and return home. Before they go, they meet Pierre's parents for a meal in a restaurant. On the way, Pierre's friend Tom wants to post his cards.

Je voudrais quatre timbres pour des cartes postales pour l'Angleterre.
Zhuh voo-dray kah-truh tam-bruh poor day kart poss-tahl poor lon-gler-tair.
I would like four stamps for postcards to England.

Ça fait deux euros, s'il vous plaît.
Sah fay duhz err-oh, see voos play.
That's two euros, please.

Now that Tom has posted his cards, they can all go on to the restaurant.

Est-ce-que vous avez de la place pour huit personnes?
Ay-ser-kuh vooz av-ay duh lah plass poor weet pair-song?
Do you have a table for eight people?

Oui, avec plaisir.
Suivez-moi, s'il vous plaît.
Wee, ah-vek play-zeer.
Swee-vay mwah, see-voo-play.
Yes, with pleasure.
Please follow me.

All the children are hungry and can't wait to order their food.

Je peux prendre votre commande?
Zhuh puh pron-druh vott-ruh kom-ond?
Can I take your order?

Oui, nous sommes prêts à commander.
Wee, noo som pray ah kom-ond-ay.
Yes, we are ready to order.

Voulez-vous autre chose?
Voo-lay voo zote-ruh shows?
Would you like anything else?

Non, merci. Ça suffit.
Nong, mair-see. Sah soo-fee.
No, thank you. That's enough.

53

A day out

The Bernard family is back home again. Monsieur Bernard is at work but François and Nicole are on holiday from school. Madame Bernard takes them to the tourist information centre to look for things to do.

Les grottes sont ouvertes tous les jours?
Lay grott song too-vairt too lay zhoor?
Are the caves open every day?

Oui, madame, à partir de dix heures jusqu'à cinq.
Wee, mad-ahm, ah pah-teer duh dee zerr zhoo-skah sank.
Yes, madam, from 10 o'clock until five.

Moi, je préfère visiter le château.
Mwah, zhuh pray-fair vee-zee-tay luhr shat-oh.
I'd rather visit the castle.

Non, je préfère le cinéma. J'adore les dessins animés.
Nong, zhuh pray-fair luh see-nay-mah. Zhad-or lay des-sang zan-ee-may.
No, the cinema. I love cartoons.

Allons au château cet après-midi, et au cinéma ce soir.
Al-long zoh shat-oh set ap-pray-mee-dee, aytoh see-nay-mah ser swahr.
Let's go to the castle this afternoon and the cinema this evening.

54

la glace *lah glas* ice cream • la sucette *lah soo-set* lollipop • la pièce *lah pee-yes* coin

Sleepover

Nicole's school friend, Aimée, wants her to go and spend the night at her house. Her mother, Madame Picquet, phones Madame Bernard.

Bonjour, Madame Bernard. Comment allez-vous?
Bong-joor, Mad-ahm Bare-nard. Comm-ong tal-ay voo?
Good morning, Mrs Bernard. How are you?

**Bonjour, Madame Picquet.
Je vais bien, merci, et vous?**
*Bong-joor, Mad-ahm Pee-kay.
Zhuh vay be-yang, mair-see. Ay voo?*
Good morning, Mrs Picquet.
I'm well, thank you, and you?

**Aimée voudrait inviter Nicole à passer
la nuit chez nous. Est-ce-que vous êtes d'accord?**
*Ay-may voo-dray ang-vee-tay Nick-oll ah pass-ay
lah nwee shay noo. Ay-suh-kuh voo zet dak-aw?*
Aimée would like to invite Nicole
to spend the night with us.
Is that all right with you?

**Oui, Nicole acceptera
avec grand plaisir.**
*Wee, Nick-oll ak-sept-er-rah
ah-vek grong play-zeer.*
Yes, Nicole accepts
with great pleasure.

56

les petits soldats *lay puh-tee sowl-dah* **toy soldiers** • **le petit train** *luh pet-ee trang* **model train**

le midi *luh meed-ee* midday • l'après midi *lap-ray-meed-ee* afternoon

The Tour de France

Every year there is a world-famous cycling race called the Tour de France (too-er duh Fronce) which lasts for three weeks. Thousands of people watch it if it passes through their town, and millions watch on television.

L'homme en tête ressemble un peu
à Lance Armstrong!
*Lom ong tett regard ung puh
ah Lance Armstrong!*
The man in the lead looks a bit
like Lance Armstrong!

Allez! Allez!
Al-ay! Al-ay!
Come on, come on!

Illness and accidents

France has one of the best medical services in the world. If something is wrong with you, you can be treated quickly and efficiently.

J'ai mal à la tête.
Zhay mal ah lah tett.
I've got a headache.

Il faut aller voir le docteur.
Eel foe tal-ay vwahr luh dok-ter.
You must go and see the doctor.

Here are a few little things that could go wrong.

Elle a attrapé un coup de soleil.
Ell ah at-rap-ay ung koo duh soh-lay.
She is sunburned.

J'ai mal au ventre.
Zhay mal oh vong-truh.
I've got a stomach ache.

Il a de la fièvre.
Eel ah duh lah fee-ayv-ruh.
He has a fever.

Bits of me

Here are lots of useful words about you and the clothes that you wear.

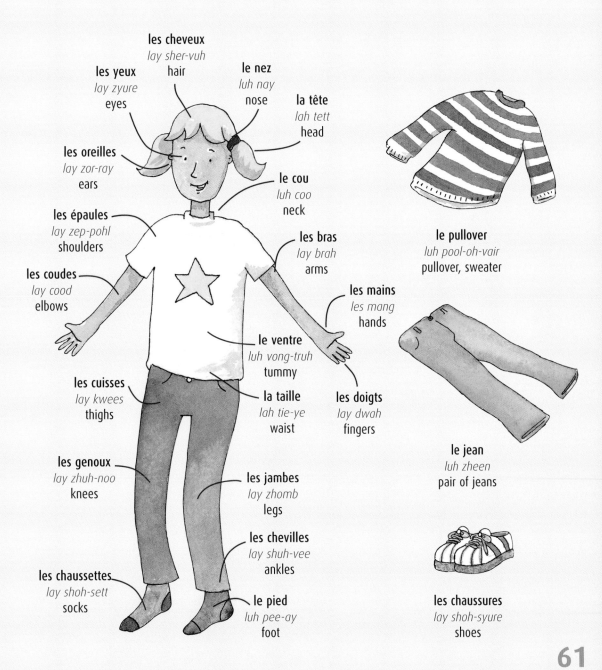

les cheveux
lay sher-vuh
hair

les yeux
lay zyure
eyes

le nez
luh nay
nose

la tête
lah tett
head

les oreilles
lay zor-ray
ears

le cou
luh coo
neck

les épaules
lay zep-pohl
shoulders

les bras
lay brah
arms

les coudes
lay cood
elbows

les mains
les mang
hands

le ventre
luh vong-truh
tummy

les cuisses
lay kwees
thighs

la taille
lah tie-ye
waist

les doigts
lay dwah
fingers

les genoux
lay zhuh-noo
knees

les jambes
lay zhomb
legs

les chevilles
lay shuh-vee
ankles

les chaussettes
lay shoh-sett
socks

le pied
luh pee-ay
foot

le pullover
luh pool-oh-vair
pullover, sweater

le jean
luh zheen
pair of jeans

les chaussures
lay shoh-syure
shoes

61

la bouche *lah boosh* mouth ● le menton *luh mong-tong* chin ● la robe *lah rob* dress ● la jupe *la zhoop* skirt

Counting

The only difficult thing about French numbers is that 70 (soixante-dix) literally means 'sixty and ten'; 80 (quatre-vingts) is 'four twenties'; and 90 (quatre-vingt-dix) is 'four twenties and ten'.

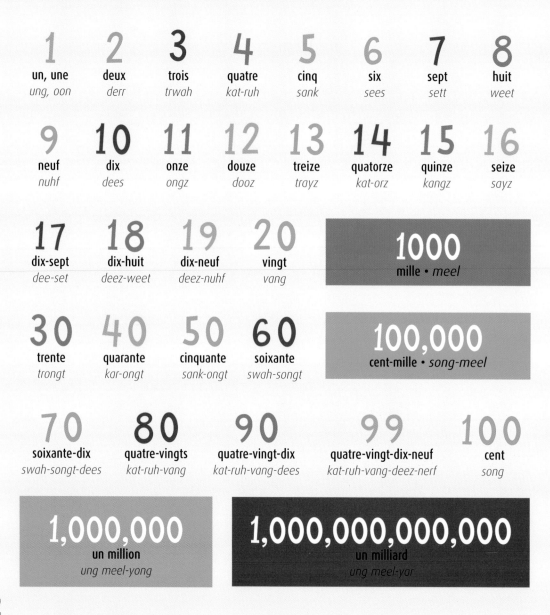

1	2	3	4	5	6	7	8
un, une	deux	trois	quatre	cinq	six	sept	huit
ung, oon	*derr*	*trwah*	*kat-ruh*	*sank*	*sees*	*sett*	*weet*

9	10	11	12	13	14	15	16
neuf	dix	onze	douze	treize	quatorze	quinze	seize
nuhf	*dees*	*ongz*	*dooz*	*trayz*	*kat-orz*	*kangz*	*sayz*

17	18	19	20
dix-sept	dix-huit	dix-neuf	vingt
dee-set	*deez-weet*	*deez-nuhf*	*vang*

1000
mille • *meel*

30	40	50	60
trente	quarante	cinquante	soixante
trongt	*kar-ongt*	*sank-ongt*	*swah-songt*

100,000
cent-mille • *song-meel*

70	80	90	99	100
soixante-dix	quatre-vingts	quatre-vingt-dix	quatre-vingt-dix-neuf	cent
swah-songt-dees	*kat-ruh-vang*	*kat-ruh-vang-dees*	*kat-ruh-vang-deez-nerf*	*song*

1,000,000
un million
ung meel-yong

1,000,000,000,000
un milliard
ung meel-yar

quart *kar* quarter • **demi** *duh-mee* half • **quatre et demi** *kat-ray duh-mee* four and a half

Telling the time

The main thing to remember about telling the time is that instead of saying so many minutes <u>before</u> the hour, the French say so many minutes <u>less</u> (moins).

Il est onze heures.
Eel ayt ongz err.
It's eleven o'clock.

Quelle heure est-il, s'il te plaît, Nicole?
Kell err ayt-eel, see-tuh-play, Nick-oll?
What's the time, please, Nicole?

Il est neuf heures exactement.
Eel ay nuhf err eggs-akt-tuh-mong.
It's exactly nine o'clock.

Il est onze heures et quart.
Eel ayt ongz err ay kahr.
It's quarter past eleven.

Il est onze heures dix.
Eel ayt ongz err dees.
It's ten past eleven.

Il est onze heures et demie.
Eel ayt ongz err ay der-mee.
It's half past eleven.

Il est onze heures moins vingt-cinq.
Eel ayt ongz err mwang vang-sank.
It's twenty-five minutes to eleven.

Il est onze heures moins le quart.
Eel ayt ongz err mwang luh kahr.
It's a quarter to eleven.

Il est minuit moins six.
Eel ay meen-wee mwang seese.
It's six minutes to midnight.

Il est midi.
Eel ay mee-dee.
It's midday (noon)
or
Il est minuit.
Eel ay meen-wee.
It's midnight.

63

Days, months and seasons

The French do not use capital letters to start days of the week, months or seasons.

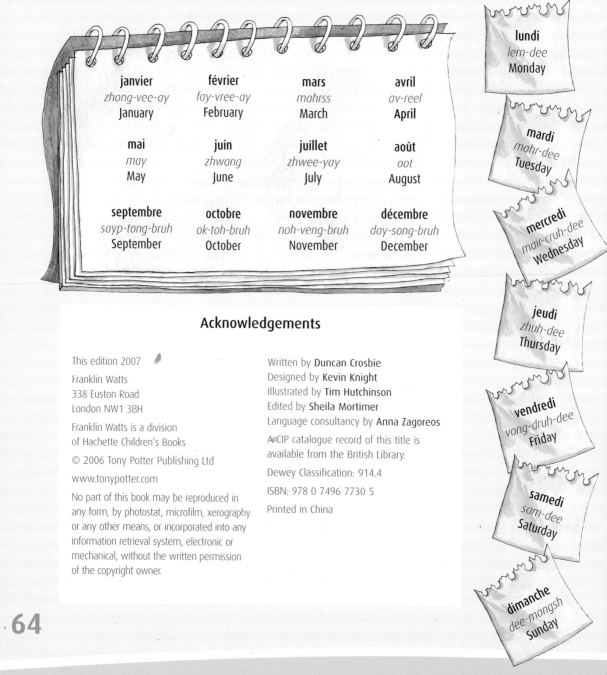

janvier
zhong-vee-ay
January

février
fay-vree-ay
February

mars
mahrss
March

avril
av-reel
April

mai
may
May

juin
zhwang
June

juillet
zhwee-yay
July

août
oot
August

septembre
sayp-tong-bruh
September

octobre
ok-toh-bruh
October

novembre
noh-veng-bruh
November

décembre
day-song-bruh
December

lundi
lern-dee
Monday

mardi
mahr-dee
Tuesday

mercredi
mair-cruh-dee
Wednesday

jeudi
zhuh-dee
Thursday

vendredi
vong-druh-dee
Friday

samedi
sam-dee
Saturday

dimanche
dee-mongsh
Sunday

Acknowledgements

This edition 2007

Franklin Watts
338 Euston Road
London NW1 3BH

Franklin Watts is a division
of Hachette Children's Books

© 2006 Tony Potter Publishing Ltd

www.tonypotter.com

No part of this book may be reproduced in
any form, by photostat, microfilm, xerography
or any other means, or incorporated into any
information retrieval system, electronic or
mechanical, without the written permission
of the copyright owner.

Written by **Duncan Crosbie**
Designed by **Kevin Knight**
Illustrated by **Tim Hutchinson**
Edited by **Sheila Mortimer**
Language consultancy by **Anna Zagoreos**

A CIP catalogue record of this title is
available from the British Library.

Dewey Classification: 914.4

ISBN: 978 0 7496 7730 5

Printed in China

La fête du travail *lar fett doo trahv-eye* May Day ● **Le quatorze juillet** *luh kat-orz zhwee-yay* Bastille Day

UNIVERSITY OF CHESTER, WARRINGTON CAMPUS